A Gift For:

From:

How to Make Your Cat an Internet Celebrity

$ $ $

A Guide to Financial Freedom

by Patricia Carlin

with photography by

Dustin Fenstermacher

QUIRK BOOKS
PHILADELPHIA

Copyright © 2014 by Quirk Productions, Inc.

Published in 2015 by Hallmark Gift Books, a division of Hallmark Cards, Inc., under license from Quirk Books.

ISBN: 978-1-59530-831-3

BOK2211

Designed and illustrated by Doogie Horner, with modifications by Hallmark.

Quirk Books

215 Church Street

Philadelphia, PA 19106

quirkbooks.com

10 9 8 7 6 5 4 3 2 1

Contents

Embracing Your Destiny

Someday, many years from now, your grandchildren will ask about your webcat fortune. "Where is it, Gran-Gran?" they'll squeak in their precious voices. "And when might we spend it?"

Will you tell them that the money is invested in a 529 college savings plan? That it's safely stashed in thousand-dollar bundles under your mattress?

Or will you be forced to admit that— despite owning both a cat and a computer during this legendary Golden Age of Cat Videos—you were the only cretin in the world who failed to cash in?

If you answered "yes" to the previous question, then this book is your financial wake-up call. Humans have always enjoyed imagery of the feline species, from the earliest cave paintings through the invention of photography. But now, thanks to the Internet, cat photos and videos can be shared like never before, even with people who don't want them.

The time to grab your slice of this furry pie is now. Actually, it's way past now because while you've been going around *not* getting rich off your cat, the Web has been populated with the likes of Ceiling Cat, Maru, Li'l Bub, and Grumpy Cat. Their owners already understand the guiding principle of the twenty-first-century global economy, which can be summed up in a single sentence:

No financial opportunity will give you a greater return on investment than your cat.

Don't believe me? Take a look at the current economy and ask yourself: Where else can my money deliver a higher return? The stock market? Please. Mutual funds? You don't even know what those are. A "savings account"? What are you, an eight-year-old with his first bank book? It's time to get serious about your future. If you're not putting every cent you have into making your cat an Internet sensation, you are digging yourself into a financial hole that will one day become your own grave.

Now, you're probably thinking, "I'm not a Wall Street investor. I'm just an ordinary dope who always puts in my ATM card backward." That may be true, but there's no reason you can't expect to achieve staggeringly unlikely results by tapping into your pet cat's innate money-generating potential. You don't have to be a financial genius like Jimmy Buffett. Your cat doesn't have to be talented, smart, or even pleasant to look at. In fact, you can take your cat's worst physical and behavioral flaws and market them as publicity hooks.

This road won't be easy. In fact, it won't even be a road; it'll be more like a trail of urine that you can see only with an ultraviolet lamp. You'll face unique cat-related hazards, like cat scratch fever, cat fights, secondhand hairballs, and irritable yowl syndrome. And because your cat is, in all likelihood, a lazy creature who likes to sleep most of the time, you'll have to work twice as hard for the both of you (which adds up to four times as hard). You'll need to be a talent scout, a publicist, a savvy producer, a keen-eyed director, a somewhat competent editor, and a save-all-receipts manager if you want your cat to become a revenue-generating meme.

It's definitely a lot of work. But picture yourself at a cocktail party, reeling off the number of views your latest clip has received while all the other millionaires spit out their drinks in disbelief. It will be so worth it.

CHAPTER 1

Grooming Your Star

You think you know your cat. But do you? Gerald Wenderson of Bayonne, New Jersey, thought he knew his kitty Chalky pretty well. But then one day he saw his chubby, gray, shorthaired feline napping on a blue blanket, and an idea was born. Now Cloud Cat has become a beloved Internet meme, Photoshopped into the skies from Hong Kong to Hackensack. Surely you're familiar with his famous catchphrase, "Meow's the weather down there?" And I'm certain that your cat possesses some special talent or freakish attribute that can propel him into the stratosphere. All you need to do is find it.

How to Identify Your Cat's Special Gifts: The OBISTPHYBEHO System

What's the easiest way to identify your cat's special gifts? Just memorize this simple acronym: OBISTPHYBEHO. It stands for OBserve, Identify, STudy, PHYsical, BEhavioral, HOnesty. Here's how the system works:

Step 1. OBSERVE. Assess your feline's potential by taking a long hard look at him. Place your cat in a well-lit room. Study him from all angles, moving slowly so as not to trigger a startled reaction. You should know this cat well enough to pick him out of a police lineup (and don't think that scenario won't ever happen).

Step 2. IDENTIFY your cat's most noteworthy features. You'll have to ask hard questions. What makes your cat meme-worthy? Why would a complete stranger want to immortalize this animal on a Facebook wall? Remember, your cat will be vying with hedgehogs, pandas, babies, and Bible quotes for that same space. What does she bring to the table? Jot down anything that comes to mind: dreamy eyes, a mellifluous meow, a two-tone coat, the ability to fart while eating.

Step 3. STUDY the notes from Step 2. Do they make any sense at all? Are you even *taking* notes? If not, repeat steps 1 and 2.

Step 4. Focus on the PHYSICAL. Consider your cat as if he was a physical object; a delicate sculpture perhaps, or a pile of sweat socks. What are his best angles? Does he even have angles? Are most of his flaws confined to one side of the body? Does your cat need dental work, a haircut, or perhaps a bath?

Step 5. Focus on the BEHAVIORAL. It's not only the way a cat looks that makes her famous; it's also the way she acts. This may be the hardest assessment to make since, 99% of the time, most cats don't do anything. Or do they? Take a closer look . . . perhaps her whiskers twitch in a funny way when she yawns. Maybe her tail taps out the rhythm to Ravel's *Bolero.* When guests come over, is there something she does that visitors find fascinating? For instance, do they comment on the cat's resemblance to Agnes Moorehead, her cute way of chewing on extension cords, or perhaps her hostile reaction to being touched? Hollywood uses focus groups all the time to test what works.

In the world of feline fame, seemingly negative characteristics can be a ticket to wildly disproportionate success.

You can, too, just by luring a small group of trusted acquaintances to your home and keeping them in a room with your cat for several hours. Take notes.

Step 6. Employ HONESTY. It's quite possible that your emotional attachment to this creature may blind you to your cat's relative lack of pizzazz. You think you've got a super cutie-pie, but in fact what you have is a gargoyle. You view your pet as a Stephen Hawking–level supergenius, when in truth he couldn't think his way out of a paper bag (literally). But take heart! In the world of feline fame, seemingly negative characteristics can be a ticket to wildly disproportionate success. It may be painful to acknowledge that your cat is hideous, clumsy, or unpleasant. But none of that means he can't make bank.

It's sometimes difficult to be critical of someone you love (even if that someone stalks and kills innocent songbirds for fun). So read on to learn how you can determine your cat's particular skill set. Figure that out, and you're one step closer to needing brand-new dreams, because the old ones have all come true.

Who's Your Tabby?
Identifying Your Cat's Type

There are many ways for a cat to achieve lasting fame. The key is understanding what sort of role your cat was born to play on the grand stage of Internet life, what archetype she most deeply resonates with, what niche she can comfortably settle into (after kneading it with her paws for twenty minutes). In short, her type. On the following page you'll find a scientifically plausible list of all possible cat types—that is, all the ones with financial potential—including the distinguishing characteristics that will help you pigeonhole your feline into the proper category.

IS YOUR CAT A SWEET BABY KITTEN?

- **Would you describe the cat as "fuzzy"?**
- **Does the cat approach even mundane objects with wonder?**
- **Is it hard to maintain your customary cynicism in the presence of the cat?**

Managing the Sweet Baby Kitten: Handle this cat gently. He's young and impressionable, perhaps unprepared for the brutal world of social media. Also, his bones are not completely fused together.

On the other hand, cha-ching! The camera *loves* kittens. Your footage will practically sell itself. But the shelf life of the sweet, sweet baby cat is quite short, so record as much video as possible before this little fellow loses his looks. Not all cats age well, and it is the rare kitten who can continue working through puberty.

How to film the Sweet Baby Kitten: To highlight the cat's utter cuteness, use household objects to emphasize his small stature. Try placing him in a shot glass, a shirt pocket, a tube sock, or a Baby Björn. You might also emphasize his poor motor skills and overall weakness. Cover him entirely with a handkerchief. Can he free himself? Finally, try emphasizing the sweet baby kitten's general inexperience with the world around him. Fire up the webcam as you introduce him to the wonder of: Windows. Dogs. Running water. Shadows.

CANDY

BUDDHA
BELLY

IS YOUR CAT A LAZY BUM?

- **Have you ever checked your cat's pulse?**
- **Does the cat refuse to eat food on the far side of his plate?**
- **Do rodents scamper freely on and around the cat?**

Managing the Lazy Bum: Don't mistake this cat for a loser; you just need to learn a few tips to make your cat's inertia work *for* you. You might market your cat as someone who's living the dream, a feline Lebowski "takin' 'er easy for all us sinners." Working stiffs everywhere will vicariously enjoy the loafing and goldbricking he so clearly embodies. Or perhaps he's more of a Buddha figure, an enlightened being who has realized the value of stillness and peace. He could be an inspiration to all of us who long to escape the hectic pace of modern life.

How to film the Lazy Bum: Test the limits of his nonchalance by provoking him with different stimuli and gauging his reaction. Possibilities include a jack-in-the-box, bubbles, techno music, a spider monkey (if you can't get one, just use a spider plant and wave the leaves around), chattering wind-up teeth, your grandmother, a Chucky doll, Gregorian chant, a chain saw. The beauty of this approach is that if the cat does react, you have a winning video—but if he does not, you have begun a challenge that could engage your audience for months to come.

IS YOUR CAT A TOTAL BADASS?

- **Does the cat swagger?**
- **If you try to pet him, will he draw blood?**
- **Has he ever shoved *you* off the couch?**

Managing the Total Badass: Understand that a badass cat doesn't have to be big and beefy; Chuck Norris is only 5'10." The key concepts here are presence and intimidation. Your cat's version of Chuck Norris's roundhouse kick might be hissing, staring, stretching, uninvited lap sitting, and/or refusing to step aside when you encounter him on the stairs. Capture these moves for the viewing public and there's money to be made (though be warned: it may only make the cat's attitude worse).

How to film the Total Badass: The badass cat needs someone, or some thing, to act badass toward. So surround him with other animals (if they have nervous conditions that accentuate his menacing qualities, so much the better). Present him with situations that he should, by all rights, fear, but that you know will just push his buttons: a trip to the vet, a child's birthday party, a Roomba. Film yourself trying to trim his claws or load him into a cat carrier. Accessorize him with a shoulder holster or a sleeveless T-shirt. Film yourself trying to get those things on him.

TOTAL
BADASS

use a zoom lens
so you won't
have to get
too close.

DOO

DAREDEVIL!

Hire sportscasters
to provide
commentary
during her stunts.

OMG

HIGH

LOW

IS YOUR CAT A DAREDEVIL?

- **Does the cat walk upright, even occasionally?**
- **Is she the first thing you think of when you hear the sound of breaking glass?**
- **Do you frequently find her in places impossible to reach?**

Managing the Daredevil: Your cat is an adrenaline junkie, and each stunt that she survives sets the bar ever higher for her twisted idea of kicks. Awesome! Her drive for creative danger is going to make your job that much easier. But be aware that spontaneity is a big part of this cat's free-wheeling lifestyle, so you'll want to be ready at a moment's notice to capture the action. The downside? The daredevil cat's high risk of injury or death. A tiny crash helmet may help (or may just be adorable). You'll want to purchase adequate death and disability coverage for this animal. It's tax deductible (perhaps).

How to film the Daredevil: Create some classic daredevil tableaus and see what happens. For example, place ten soda cans in an orderly line. Situate a cat-sized toy motorcycle at one end. Position your camera to capture the entire panorama. Record as the daredevil cat runs into the frame, knocks over the motorcycle and cans, leaps onto the drapes, climbs to the ceiling, and flips over backward to land on the ceiling fan.

IS YOUR CAT A CLOWN?

- **Do other cats seem to find your cat hilarious?**
- **Do mundane tasks, like jumping onto a windowsill, inevitably propel the cat into a series of increasingly outrageous pratfalls?**
- **Does he take after Harlequin, Pantalone, or any of the commedia dell'arte character types?**

Managing the Clown: With their mysterious demeanor and subtle ways, it's easy to believe that cats exist on a higher metaphysical plane than human beings. Until one does something to convince you otherwise, like spend forty minutes trying to escape from a cereal box. Yes, good times abound with the funny cat. But remember, good times won't pay the rent. So don't spend so much time laughing at the cat trying to lift an ice cube with his paws that you forget to capture the comic magic on video.

How to film the Clown: Physical comedy is this cat's forte, so go with it. Place him in an environment replete with items he can interact with, react to, or trip over: toilet paper rolls, a spool of yarn, a wading pool filled with marbles. For good measure, try leaving a banana cream pie on the counter, or positioning a banana peel where he might slip on it.

BOING!
funny ear
CLOWN
funny whiskers
HAHAHA!
YOINK!
funny tongue

COMPLETE MORON

DUM

DUM

DUM

- Be careful where he sticks his head.
- Will eat rubber bands.
- Beware accidental electrocution.

IS YOUR CAT A COMPLETE MORON?

- **Do you constantly have to remind the cat who you are?**
- **Has the cat ever eaten from his litter box?**
- **Does he have trouble pronouncing the word "meow"?**

Managing the Complete Moron: When you decided to adopt a cat, you expected to share your life with a higher order of animal. A creature sharper than, say, a hamster or a basset hound. Unfortunately, no species is without embarrassing specimens. We humans have Donald Trump. The feline community has . . . your cat. I ask you, which species has been brought lower? Fortunately lack of intellect is no barrier to success! The public loves dumb stars (can't think of an example right now), so your lovable lunkhead is all but assured of a fine career.

How to film the Complete Moron: Your best bet is to emphasize his uncatlike qualities, such as clumsiness, poor grooming, or fear of mice. Encourage any charming quirks, like a tendency to be startled by his own tail. Place him in situations where he is likely to commit a gaffe, such as stepping on another cat's head or trying to lick his own reflection. Pit him against a highly skilled cat in contests, including ping-pong ball swatting, string play, and eluding small children.

IS YOUR CAT A HEARTTHROB?

- **Do cats of the same sex wanna be your cat, while cats of the opposite sex wanna get with your cat?**
- **Does the cat get away with bloody murder simply because you don't have the heart to discipline him?**
- **Do you suspect people spend time with you only to get close to your cat?**

Managing the Heartthrob: Don't hate him because he's beautiful. Your cat has been graced with the face of an angel and the body of a cuddly toy. He's won the genetic lottery . . . and you, his owner, have won yourself a ticket on the gravy train. Enjoy the ride! Ticket price: regular hair, nail, and whisker maintenance.

Never forget: Your cat's good looks = your nest egg.

How to film the Heartthrob: Set this creature up with his own YouTube channel and then sit back and watch the "likes" pile up. Soon after, the endorsement deals will start rolling in. Be sure to associate the cat with only wholesome products, so as not to cheapen his image. Just kidding! Grab whatever $$$ comes your way. However, should the cat become entangled in a committed relationship, keep it on the down-low. You want every viewer to fantasize that this feline has eyes for her alone.

Heartthrob
xoxo

SO DREAMY! ♡

OMG!

SQUEEE! ♡

— DON'T SKIMP ON HAIR AND WHISKER STYLING. ♡

SCARY UGLY BEAST

- horrific screen presence
- hard to tell if it's actually a cat
- add ominous soundtrack to video

NIGHTMARE FUEL

IS YOUR CAT A SCARY UGLY BEAST?

- **Since owning the cat, has your appetite significantly decreased?**
- **Does the cat's face lack symmetry, two eyes, or fur?**
- **Has the cat ever been mistaken for a chupacabra?**

Managing the Scary Ugly Beast: When nature accidentally produces a monstrosity, society usually corrects the mistake by drowning the creature at birth. If those checks and balances fail, the world teeters on the edge of aesthetic ruin. What good is a gorgeous natural tableau if it's studded with hideous wildlife? Even Thoreau would agree. But your cat somehow beat the system; good on her. And fortunately even the most grotesque cat can have a long and successful Internet career. In the same way that we enjoy a horror film or a KISS reunion tour, we enjoy looking at your cat and being frightened. Just so long as we can turn off the monitor and make her go away.

How to film the Scary Ugly Beast: Take advantage of the revulsion your cat inspires by simply walking her down a busy street. Record the candid reactions of passersby. Walk past a schoolyard at recess. Capture the screams. Or try re-creating moments from classic horror movie scenes with your cat as the villain: *Psycho* shower scene (cat as Bates); *Silence of the Lambs* (cat as Lecter); *Elephant Man* (cat as Merrick).

IS YOUR CAT CLINICALLY INSANE?

- **Does the cat appear to obey unseen forces?**
- **Does she attempt to climb trees that aren't there?**
- **Does she look at you like *you're* the crazy one?**

Managing the Clinically Insane Cat: Life with an unbalanced cat is never boring. And even the unbalanced cat can carve out a career in the world of feline videography, if you manage her carefully. After all, show business is full of colorful folks like Charlie Sheen, Crispin Glover, and Randy Quaid. They get work, so why shouldn't your cat?

How to film the Clinically Insane Cat: You'll need to keep a closed set to contain this cat's fragile nerves. Do not overscript the action—simply let your cat's crazy train-wreck behavior unfold in a natural, gawker-friendly way. The best approach is documentary-style. Think *Grey Gardens* or *March of the Penguins*: grotesque, Grand Guignol theater, with not much embellishment necessary. Insert postproduction commentary from an animal psychologist.

> *Life with an unbalanced cat is never boring.*

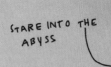

STARE INTO THE ABYSS

CLINICALLY
INSANE

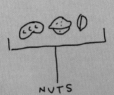

NUTS

— Consult an animal psychologist as needed.

IS YOUR CAT UTTERLY BLAND?

- **Do you sometimes forget you own a cat?**
- **Are you unable to remember what the cat looks like if he's not sitting in front of you?**
- **Do squirrels or sparrows fail to react when the cat crosses their path?**

Managing the Utterly Bland Cat: Your pet may be unremarkable in every way, but that doesn't mean there's no work for him. His lack of standout features can become his most valuable asset. He's the Everycat, the feline mirror in which we see our own lives reflected. He's also easy to transform with a little creative thinking. Try lifting the cat by his armpits—is he longer than you expected? Look, everybody, it's Longcat! (Creative camera placement can enhance this concept.) Add extra sizzle by giving your cat a signature accessory, like an eye patch, a vest, or a jaunty beret (more about using props and costumes in the next section).

How to film the Utterly Bland Cat: Try placing this cat in an ensemble situation; adding a toddler or a dog to the mix will reduce the pressure on the cat to carry the whole show. Or consider hiring a writer to draft an interior monologue for this cat. You (or an actor) voice over what the cat is "thinking."

Kitty Allure: How Accessories Make Your Cat Stand Out

Imagine yourself at a casting call. The waiting room is crowded with dozens of (insert an adjective that describes your pet's look) cats and their (insert an adjective that describes you) managers. Except for their collars, all these cats are identical. But wait! One kitty is holding a cello case. Does he play? From which academy of music did he graduate? Who is this mysterious feline? Sensing the excitement, the casting director quickly ushers this artistic creature inside, dismissing the other losers without a second glance.

Wow. A skill like that (or even the appearance of one) really gives a performer a competitive advantage! It's a powerful example of how, by investing a little more time and energy, you can give your cat not just a look, but a big juicy chunk of *character*. Now, you're probably used to thinking of character as something that takes a lifetime to build. And that may be true, if you just knocked a baseball through the window of your elderly neighbor's house, denied it, and are having a heart-to-heart talk with your dad. But in the high-stakes world of Internet cat videos, character basically boils down to one word: props.

But where, you ask, might one acquire a cat-sized cello? From a Harry Whittier Frees estate sale? Sure, but those are few and far between. Reader, you are about to discover the best-kept secret in feline entertainment management: THE AMERICAN GIRL STORE. This place is a veritable treasure trove of kitty props and set decoration, not to mention costuming!

For those of you without small children, let me explain: American Girl is a popular brand of dolls depicting girls from various historical periods. But forget about the dolls. Cat managers flock to these stores because of the vast assortment of clothing and accessories available, all perfectly sized for the domestic housecat! It's like visiting a parallel universe where everything is adorable in scale. No more carving tiny accordions from soap; simply walk right in and buy one (or order online). Does this sound like cheating? Remember that without his little pickax, sifting pan, and sluices, Internet sensation Miner Forty-Niner Cat would be just another tabby sitting in the mud.

Remember that without his little pickax, sifting pan, and sluices, Internet sensation Miner Forty-Niner Cat would be just another tabby sitting in the mud.

THE PROP	THE CHARACTER
Tiny ski chalet	Professional stunt-skier
Adorable cat-sized crutches	Recuperating tap-dance accident survivor
Teeny hot-air balloon	Phileas Fogg
Pint-sized VW Beetle	Cheech or Chong
Petite camera and flash	Depression-era cub reporter and opium addict
Eensy-weensy weaving loom	Sweatshop worker
Darling little science lab	Madame Curie
Miniature baby grand piano	Duke Ellington

jazz singer

ballerina

pirate

reindeer

Here are just a few of the possibilities.

These kinds of props not only create visual interest, they instantly generate rich and unique storylines you can use in your videos. This is a foolproof way to build lasting fame for your pet, whose actual life is probably not very interesting.

Does My Cat Need a Stage Name?

In a word, probably. Many cat owners suffer from a crippling lack of originality when it comes to pet nomenclature. No big deal if your cat isn't working, but cats with star ambition need every advantage.

CAT COLOR	white	gray	black
GOOD NAMES	Snowball	Smoky	Blackie
	Snowflake	Shadow	Midnight
	Snow White	Misty	Inky
	Snowy	Grayson	Boo
	Blanca	Ashes	Jinx
	Casper	Dusty	Lucky
	Coke	Stormy	Ace
BETTER NAMES	Ghostface Killah	Earl Grey	Noirman

Ziggy Stardust

The Preacher

Lady Marmalade

orange	calico	any color	black & white
Tiger	Callie	Kitty	Oreo
Tigger	Calvin	Tom	Tuxedo
Ginger	Patches	Whiskers	Felix
Morris	Spot	Socks	Sylvester
Rusty	Kallie	Boots	Penguin
Garfield	Cally	Mittens	B.W.
Sunshine	Kali, Goddess of Death	Max	Zebra
Blorange	Bubbles	Hulk	Cookie-Puss

Changing your cat's name is easy enough. There's little paperwork involved, and in all likelihood your pet is completely unaware she even has a name. The challenge, of course, is coming up with a moniker that's catchy and unforgettable, so full of zazz that it will go viral like a cold sore at a make-out party. Here are a few tricks that product marketers, talent agents, and best-selling authors use to generate marquee-worthy names.

Translate your cat's current name into French.

This instantly creates an air of sophistication, mystery, and ennui: Adds class, doesn't it? *Très magnifique*. (That would also make a great cat name!)

Smoky = **Enfumé**

Shadow = **Ombre**

Boots = **Bottes**

Socks = **Chaussettes**

Bastard = **Bâtard**

Clawed = **Claude**

Morris = **Maurice**

Tom = **Tom**
(pronounced with a French accent)

Spanish works, too!

Only Mandarin has more native speakers than Spanish, so you're giving the cat immediate worldwide appeal. (You could try a Mandarin name, but I assume a tonal language is beyond your abilities.)

El Tigre = **Tiger**
Solana = **Sunshine**
Féliz = **Felix**
Sanguinario = **Bloodthirsty**
Descarado = **Saucy**
La Bamba = **Da Bomb**
Salsa = **Sauce**
Perro = **Dog**

Or try a phonetic spelling.

Simply rewrite an existing name as if you were a six-year-old in a spelling bee. The pronunciation remains the

L. Teegray
Mit-enz
Jinjur
Khit-tee
Bütz

same, so this is a good tactic if you don't want to have to remember a new word.

Why not add flair with special characters?

Thanks to countless hours of texting and password invention, we've learned to use alphanumeric characters that our grandparents could only dream of. So reach beyond the plain ol' ABZzzzs when compiling your pet's new alias. Hip-hop artists do this all the time, and look how popular they are. For example, consider these variations on a typical, boring cat moniker.

$hadow

Sh@d0

S|-|a:D()\/\/

S#4<0

:X{

Or try a name that's already working.

Why reinvent the wheel when it's already been reinvented several times over? True, the Screen Actors Guild forbids an actor from using another actor's name. But guess what? Your cat will never have a SAG card anyway. So go ahead—grab a name that's preloaded with star power and suck as much fame juice out of it as you can.

Tom Cruise
Brad Pitt
Justin Bieber
Lindsay Lohan
Snoop Dogg
Joe Biden
Eli Whitney
Larry Fine
Mohandas Gandhi

CHAPTER 2

Lights, Kitty, Action!

By this point, you have transformed a dull, mundane animal that nobody would look at twice into a burgeoning star, an otherworldly creature so overflowing with charm that complete strangers can barely contain themselves in the animal's presence. They say God doesn't make mistakes, but you remixed one of His less impressive B-sides and came up with a killer track worthy of prime-time airplay. It's amazing, isn't it? Now you know how Don Kirshner felt when he "discovered" the Archies.

Well, now you're going to accomplish something even greater. Something that Don Kirshner never did, and not just because the Archies broke up over artistic differences. You're going to film a hit viral video. So let's get up to speed on some basic video techniques, and quickly, before your neighbor with the one-eyed Cornish rex turns No Depth Perception Cat into a worldwide sensation.

Equipment Check

"Which camera should I use?" you ask. And I answer: How the hell should I know? This isn't *Consumer Reports*. Besides, do you really want to read about f-stops and megapixels? Doubt it. Suffice to say that many of today's smartphones capture great video, and there are digital cameras and camcorders that will fit any budget. Get advice from your nephew, or that nerdy guy who's always staring at you at work. Frankly, it's more important to use a camera that's easy for you to operate than to find one with all the latest bells and whistles. But if you like to use fancy-schmancy equipment that goes beyond what the average clod can operate, try renting your gear until you find something with the right combination of utility and snob value.

Once you have camera in hand, here's how you prep it:

Clean the lens. Use a soft dry towelette or the hem of your shirt.

Charge the camera. And keep the charger (or extra batteries) at the ready. It's likely your cat will finally behave in an interesting way just as you run out of juice.

Stabilize the camera. Use a tripod, or place the camera on something stable like a tabletop or a Canadian. True, lots of movies use a "shaky camera" effect to achieve a raw, amateur look. But your footage will be plenty amateur enough.

Test the sound system. Some microphones are better than others. Experiment to find out how close you need to be to capture the best sound. By the way, do you even know where the microphone is? Make sure you don't block it with your finger. And don't forget, your voice is liable to drown out everything else. Nix the monologue, Spaulding Gray, and let your star do the vocalizing.

Planning the Shoot

It's tempting to think that movie making is simply a matter of switching on a camera and letting things happen. That may work for a mom recording her kid's soccer game, or for Robert Altman. But film is a director's medium. You are the artist, the screen is your canvas, and you have just one brush. A brush that will spend all its time licking its own foot if you don't take control. So here's what you do.

Dress the set. Look through the camera's viewfinder and see your home through the eyes of a stranger. Anything incongruous, distracting, disturbing, or confusing—aside from your backflipping tabby—must go. Does that mean repainting the living room in earth tones and buying

YES

NO

Good set dressing: classy decor, throw pillows, primary colors.

Bad set dressing: Cat is barely visible. Move the horse.

generic self-assembled furniture from a Scandinavian warehouse store? Well, sure, that's a sensible idea. Or you can just shove your tear-gas canisters and taxidermy station to one corner of the apartment so they'll be out of the shot. Or throw blankets over everything.

Frame your shot. Next time you're watching TV—you know, that thing you used to watch before the Internet—notice where the action is during a favorite program or commercial. At the very top? No. All the way to the extreme left? Nope. Dead center? Wrong. Even the blandly competent cinematographers of *The Bold and the Beautiful* are aware of a little thing called "The Rule of Thirds." And you, too, can benefit from this strategy, which dictates where to place the action to create a dynamic shot that draws your viewer into the scene like a glue-sniffer in an envelope factory. It's easy:

1. Look into the viewfinder or screen of your camera.
2. Mentally draw vertical and horizontal lines dividing the screen into vertical and horizontal thirds.
3. Place the camera so that the cat is located where the lines intersect. If the cat moves, move the camera accordingly.

Let there be lighting. Cat videos are best shot in a controlled environment, which usually means an indoor setting from which the animal can't escape. The downside is that you lose access to natural sunlight, which is not only free but also extremely flattering and appealing (though, to be fair, it can also give you cancer). Not to worry. With a few extension cords and floor lamps, you can illuminate even the dimmest recesses of your home. For some cameras, bright lighting allows you to narrow the aperture, which means that a wider depth of field can stay in focus. My God, you see how boring camera talk can be?

Silence unwanted sounds. "Quiet on the set" is a phrase you should be ready to bust out at a moment's notice—except that it will only elicit blank stares from any clueless non-show-business types in the room. So arm yourself with a few stock phrases applicable to your particular milieu, such as "Zip your lid," "Can it," "Shut your word hole," "Silence, I tell you," and so on. Better yet, remove all extraneous loudmouths from the set, including spouses and parents.

Directing the Talent

From Orson Welles onward, every great Hollywood director has understood that you cannot direct a cat; that's why the overwhelming majority of motion pictures are built to showcase human performers instead of kittens. The best you can hope to do is trigger your cat's natural charm and/or freak factor, then capture it on camera during the few fleeting seconds when the animal's genius evinces itself in an intuitively entertaining manner. The result, if you're lucky, will be the *Citizen Kane* of Internet cat videos.

But what if your feline seems preoccupied with staring at some invisible object in the corner of the ceiling? In that case, you must prod your cat toward greatness by any means necessary. Here are some ideas to get the ball rolling.

Get Your Do-Nothing Cat to Do Something: 27 Prompts for Cinematic Glory

1. BOXES

Cats are universally drawn to boxes of any size or shape because feline wombs are made of cardboard. This behavior stems from a subconscious urge to return to the fetal state (despite the fact that a cat's life outside the womb isn't all that different from life inside it).

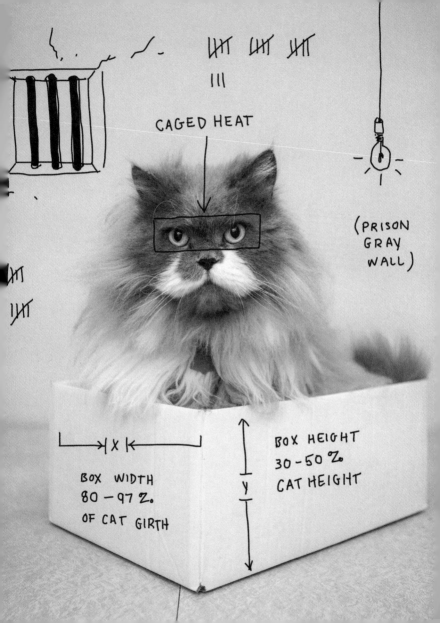

CAGED HEAT

HHT HHT HHT
III

(PRISON
GRAY
WALL)

BOX HEIGHT
30 - 50 %
CAT HEIGHT

BOX WIDTH
80 - 97 %
OF CAT GIRTH

X

Y

Simply place an empty box on the ground and your cat will step inside, not to emerge for several hours. Try labeling the box in a humorous way: TIME OUT, DO NOT DISTURB, OCCUPIED, RETURN TO SENDER, or CAUTION: CONTENTS MAY HAVE SHIFTED DURING SHIPPING are all hilarious ideas. (Don't have a box handy? A paper bag works just as well.)

2. STRING

This is a classic, and there's a reason why: the string can't fight back. So what you have is a natural-born killer cutting loose, using every lethal weapon in its arsenal against an enemy whose only defense is to dangle. Everyone loves a one-sided fight! Just be sure you use proper string deployment tactics:

1. Dangle a length of string. If cat fails to pounce, dangle string furiously.
2. Continue until cat attacks string.
3. Let cat wrestle string for 60 seconds.
4. Release string. Wait for cat to lose interest.
5. Repeat steps 1 through 4.

3. BABY

Use a crawling-type baby for best results. The walking ones are just too difficult to work with. Place the cat and the baby in close proximity, and then watch the fireworks! Baby mauls cat, cat spits and hisses cutely. Advise cat in baby talk, "No bite!" and "No scratch baby!" Did you remember to trim the cat's claws fist? Do that.

WATCH FOR POOP

TENSION

WATCH FOR CLAWS

[HUMOR]

?

[DANGER]

$ $

4. BIRD

If you can acquire a small-to medium-sized bird for little or no money, do so. Cat/bird videos are basically thrillers, a genre second only to romantic comedies in popularity. To use a bird, simply place him in a room with a drowsy cat. Birds are typically hugely annoying animals, and what you will record is an exercise in feline tolerance. You can bank on the bird squawking, trilling, and pecking at the cat with his beak. The question is, how much will the cat take? Tune in to find out!

5. CONTAINER OF TREATS

For this one you'll need a box or bucket of cat treats that is clearly marked "TREATS" (do the lettering yourself). Place the bucket on a shelf the cat can reach, but not without some difficulty. Make sure the lid is loose. When your cat inevitably climbs up and immerses his face in the treats, enter the room and exclaim in mock surprise and consternation: "Mon Dieu, Claude! Those treats are for guests!" The startled feline is likely to tumble down and spill the entire batch of treats onto the floor— the exact opposite of what you wanted to happen! For a kicker, have a dozen or so cat extras run into the room and start munching on the scattered treats. LOLwut???!

6. BATHTUB

Consider this paradox of being a cat: They love fish, but they hate water. Is it any wonder the typical feline is both repelled and fascinated by fjords, canals,

If the action feels flat, consider turning on the showerhead.

and waterways of all sorts? Take advantage of this natural aversion by perching your cat on the edge of the tub and turning on the faucet. Capture the intensity of her gaze as she ponders her options: Should she jump in? Run away? Keep gazing? If the action feels flat, consider turning on the showerhead.

7. TELEVISION

The television may be an outdated entertainment delivery device—but to your cat, it's a window into another world. Try turning on something with feline appeal, like a PBS nature show, a documentary about cheese, or *Wide World of Yarn*. Film your cat leaping at the TV screen, swiping at it with her paw, and otherwise trying to grasp the ungraspable. We've all experienced soul-crushingly frustrating moments like that, which is why it's funny.

8. HUMAN HAIR

You will need an actor with beyond-shoulder-length hair for this one. Place the cat behind a low-backed sofa and arrange the actor on the

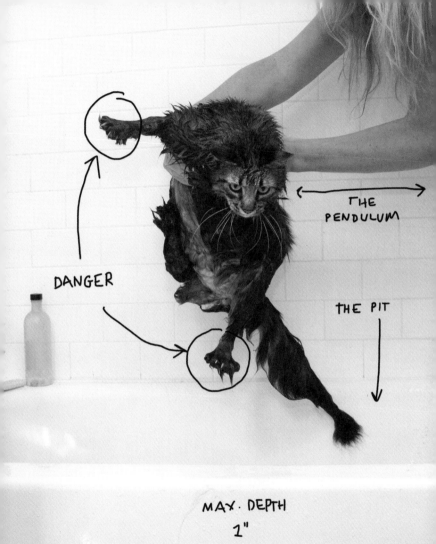

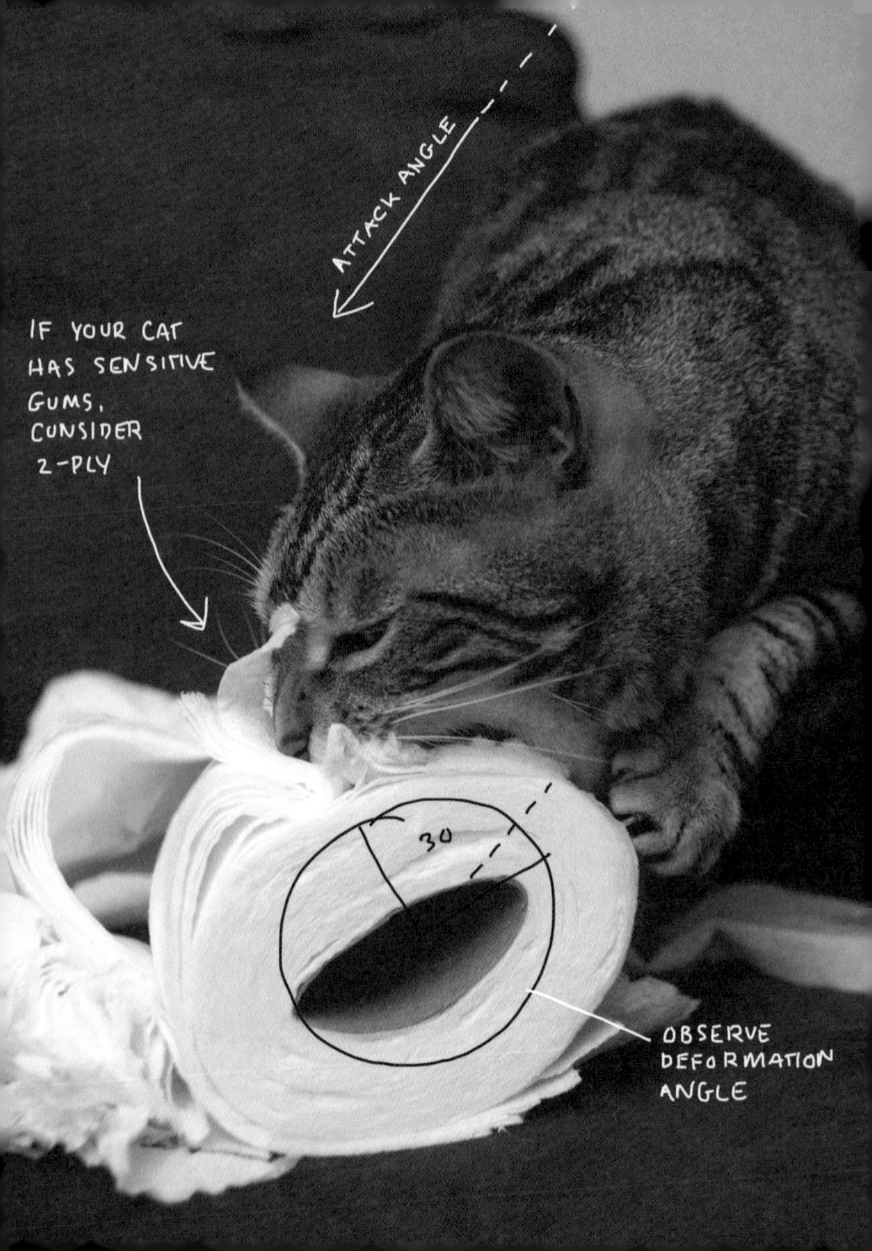
ATTACK ANGLE
IF YOUR CAT HAS SENSITIVE GUMS, CONSIDER 2-PLY
30
OBSERVE DEFORMATION ANGLE

sofa. Encourage the actor to lean back and fluff out those loose, flowing locks. (Tell the actor you're filming an ad for Pert Plus.) Zoom in on the cat as he pounces and attacks unsuspecting actor's head.

9. ROLL OF TOILET PAPER

This one works best with alert and fairly active cats—the kind who don't wait around for inanimate objects to move before pouncing on them. Place a full roll of toilet paper in a securely mounted wall dispenser. (If there's not good lighting in your bathroom, hire a contractor to install a dispenser in a well-lit area, like a vestibule or parlor.) Adjust the paper to hang over the roll. That's crucial. *It must hang over the top and front of the roll, not behind it.* Allow four squares to dangle. Watch as the cat uses both front paws to furiously spin the roll until all the paper is on the floor.

10. CEILING FAN

This is an easy one, provided you have access to a ceiling with a fan on it. Place a table directly below the ceiling fan. Place your cat on the table—oh wait, she's already there, because it's a new piece of furniture in the room. Turn the fan on low. Observe your cat flatten in suspicion at this unnatural vortex of wind. Watch her head spin as she follows the motion of the blades. Uh-oh, she looks ready to jump up at the fan . . . the perfect place to cut the video and tease for part 2.

11. PING-PONG

Of all the Olympic sports, cats have a natural flair for just one: ping-pong. Feline-style ping-pong is more like handball, if you want to get technical about it. But stop with the irrelevant tangents, because the point is there are three fantastic ways to set up a ping-pong match with your cat. And all of them produce outstanding video: Cat vs. Human, Cat vs. Cat, and Human vs. Human (with Cat interfering).

12. BUTTERFLY

Look, the typical butterfly lives for just days, sometimes even hours. And that's after a lifetime of stuffing its gullet as a gluttonous caterpillar. So you shouldn't feel bad for injecting some drama into this insect's brief and selfish life. Simply release the butterfly and record your cat as she cavorts and leaps in a vain attempt to capture the thing. If the butterfly is uncatchable, you can emancipate it back into the wild, where it will return to pollinating daffodils or whatever it is they do. And should the cat succeed, well, last time I checked there were plenty of butterflies in the world.

13. DOLLHOUSE

When you need a release from the grim realities of cat superstardom, this idea is perfect. Set up a fully furnished dollhouse. Arrange the dolls so they're, say, sitting around the dinner table. Provide their voices: "So what is it you're working on, honey? A book about cat videos? That doesn't sound very promising." "Yes, your father's right, it seems like a real waste of your time. Are you ever going back to cosmetology school? You had real talent." And then: Release your cat and have him lurch into the scene, knocking house and dolls helter-skelter. MONSTER ATTACK! WHERE'S YOUR COSMETOLOGY SCHOOL NOW, YOU LITTLE BASTARDS? So satisfying.

14. GLASS OF WATER

For the netcat impresario on a budget, this one requires no special equipment. Simply fill a tall glass with water. Place the glass beside your cat. He may test the waters with his paw, reaching into the glass and stirring the liquid to determine its viscosity. If you're lucky, he will knock the glass over, spill out almost all the water, and then insert his entire head deep into the vessel, flattening his ears against the sides and lapping at the remaining water with his tongue. That's known in the business as "glassnecking," and it's gold, baby. There are entire websites dedicated to the phenomenon!

1. The Approach

2. The Dip and Drip

3. The Flick

15. BALLOONS

For this one, you will need three to five inflated balloons, depending on the size of your cat. (Have an assistant inflate them; balloon-blower's lung is no joke, and you should take all the standard precautions.) Gently rub a balloon against your assistant's wool sweater to generate static electricity. Firmly press the balloon onto your cat's back; it should stick. Continue until the cat is fully covered with balloons. Freaking out will commence. Observe and record.

16. CHEST OF DRAWERS

For this option, you will need a chest of drawers. If you don't have a bureau available, you might try utilizing a dresser or mule chest, or perhaps a sideboard. In some cases a chifforobe might work, or a highboy. Certainly a chiffonier would be a difficult choice for this idea, but it might work in a pinch. What about a blanket chest, don't you have one of those? In any case, get a chest of drawers. You can figure out the rest yourself.

Certainly a chiffonier would be a difficult choice for this idea, but it might work in a pinch. What about a blanket chest, don't you have one of those?

17. MAN

Some cats just can't carry a whole two-minute clip (we call those cats "Persians"). If your cat is floundering, consider enlisting a human foil to shoulder some of the dramatic weight. Cat versus man is a classic conflict. Here are some failsafe ideas:

- **Man uses dust mop.** Cat perceives mop as prey and then strikes, refusing to relent. Man continues to dust.

- **Man measures carpeting.** Cat perceives tape measure as prey and then strikes, refusing to relent. Man continues to measure.

- **Man ties shoe.** Cat perceives laces as prey and then strikes, refusing to relent. Man goes with slip-ons.

- **Man reads newspaper.** Cat perceives paper as prey and then attacks, refusing to relent. Man switches to e-reader.

- **Man writes note.** Cat perceives writing implement as prey and then attacks, refusing to relent. Man signs off.

18. SHADOW

When times were tough, the wild ancestors of today's domestic cats believed they could survive just by eating the shadows of other creatures. Which is why your pet has such a strong urge to chase whatever shadow crosses her path. Simply position yourself between a light source and the cat. Rhythmically move an appendage of your choice. When you have attracted the cat's attention, increase the speed of motion. If your cat is any kind of star, she should attack that shadow as if it were a blind chipmunk she chanced upon in the yard.

19. VASE WITH IMPOSSIBLY SMALL OPENING

Place an empty vase on a table and your cat will take it as a personal challenge. Are you saying he *can't* fit inside the vase? Because he will prove you wrong. Watch as he liquefies himself before your very eyes. HE FITS! Try it again with something smaller, maybe a test tube.

GOOD

Curious cat approaches vessel.

BETTER

Face inserted. Vessel raised to upright position.

MONEY SHOT

Reality dawns in tiny cat cortex, causing cat to reassess.

20. POPCORN POPPER

This concept is an exercise in minimalism. Clear the counter, because there should be only two objects in the frame: A hot-air corn popper and a concerned cat. Like Checkhov's rifle, the popper is obviously going to play a critical role in the narrative. But how??? What??? Then, suddenly, the popping begins! All the cat can do is ineffectually swat at the domed lid with her paw. It really is like great Russian literature!

21. ROOMBA

Or any of the dozens of brands of plate-sized robotic floor cleaners that have made our lives so much easier. Simply operate the robot as directed, and your cat, if he is like all other cats in the universe, will be drawn inexplicably to the device. He may even be seized by an overwhelming desire to ride on top of the robot, cruising through your kitchen like the Pope through St. Peter's Square. Give him space. And maybe construct a little miter for him to wear as he rides.

22. FLASHLIGHT

Cats will chase shadows (see no. 18), so it only stands to reason that they would also chase the opposite of shadows, that is, light. Swirl the beam around in a darkened room. Watch how the cat contorts in his vain efforts to stop the motion. Riveting! You did remember to adjust your camera for low-light shooting, right? Great, you just wasted an hour.

23. DOGS

In every relationship, there is one who loves and one who allows himself to be loved. That's what the French say. And if they are discussing cats and dogs, they are correct. Keep one of each in your home, and the cat will inevitably shower the dog with affection. The dog will endure the affection, perhaps out of fear. Whether this is genuine fondness or some type of cat mind game is unclear. But the cute factor is off the charts! Puppies are also good.

> *Whether this is genuine fondness or some type of cat mind game is unclear.*

24. CHRISTMAS TREE

Few things are as confusing to your cat as the winter holidays. Suddenly there's a *tree* growing in the living room? WTF??? In his heightened state of perplexity, is it any wonder that he decides to climb your Christmas tree, nestle among the priceless ornaments, knock the angels from the branches, and possibly take down the entire display? Be prepared with your camera at all times, because the cat may decide to use the tree as a springboard from which to launch himself toward points he could not otherwise reach: chandeliers, china cabinets, ceiling fans, heads of visiting relatives.

25. PAPER BAG

There are few certainties in the high-stakes universe of ailurophilic entrepreneurship, but this is one: Place an empty paper bag on the floor and your cat will come. Without hesitation, she will enter the bag, scoot to the rear, and turn so that she can see out of the opening without anyone seeing her. She will remain that way for the rest of her natural life, unless and until (a) the bag is poked with a stick or (b) someone walks past the bag. When either of those things happens, BOOM! It's go-time. Cat springs into action, attacks prey (stick or person), and retreats back into bag. Elapsed time: 0.7–1.3 seconds. Cue slow-motion instant replay.

26. WALL

Cats have a tendency to believe that basic laws of gravity do not apply to them. Sometimes they're right. And sometimes they're tragically, entreatingly wrong. That's what's known in the business as "the money shot." If you are patient and/or lack the gumption to wrangle together such props as a piece of string or a friend with hair, you can certainly plunk your camera down next to a wall and wait. Sooner or later, your cat will approach the wall and hurl himself skyward in an attempt to reach a shelf or window. (Accelerate the process by taping an anchovy high up on the wall.)

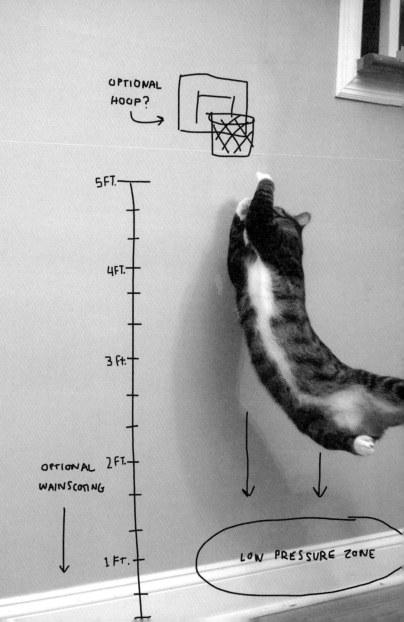

27. APP

Of course there are apps especially developed for cat interaction, but be careful—they could be potential endorsement deals. Better to save those for later and start with a human-focused app, maybe a pizza-place finder or Bejeweled Blitz. Get the camera in close as your cat reacts to the flashing graphics and peculiar sounds. Will he knock your smartphone off the table? Try to bite your iPad? Classic!

Help! My Cat Rejects These Attempts at Engagement.

If these foolproof no-fail techniques don't work, consider the time-honored technique of *féline vérité*. Set up cameras near your cat's favorite hangouts—behind the couch, in a fruit bowl, on top of another cat—and then walk away. Yes, that goes against your every instinct as a director. But all you need to do is record the animal's routine, and then later sift through the footage at your leisure to discover a revealing chronicle of this beast's hopes, dreams, and struggles. What does he do all day, this seemingly simple creature? Is he charmingly destructive? Does he have surprising moments of pathos, drama, frustration, despair? Must he summon exquisite courage just to get through the day? Does he snore?

If the answer to these questions is no, you must consider the possibility that your cat is dull. Let me ask you this: How invested are you in this particular cat? Might it be time to pawn him off to a lonely, elderly relative and get yourself a spunky kitten?

CHAPTER 3

Clawing Your Way to the Top

By now your cat has done his job as a performer. The camera's off, you've swept up the broken glass, and your star is enjoying some well-deserved downtime in a shaft of sunlight. It's all downhill from here, right? Nothing left to do but release your movie and have your mail forwarded to Easy Street.

Man, are you living in a fool's paradise. Do you think you can just go to bed early, and magical elves will come into your house at night and finish your work? The odds of that happening are very close to zero.

It's time to press on! Roll up your sleeves. If you're not wearing a shirt, put one on right now and roll the sleeves up. In fact, considering how much work is ahead of you, perhaps you should invest in a pair of old-fashioned arm suspenders to keep those sleeves up-rolled.

CROP

TWEAK

MONEMZE

Headin' for an Editin'

If you've followed the advice in this book *to the letter,* you've compiled a real gem of feline edutainment. But that treasure is a diamond in the rough. You're going to polish that diamond until you can see your own reflection, and in that reflection your eyes will reflect dollar signs back at you. And those dollar signs will be made of solid gold. Welcome to the wonderful world of *editing*. You will not only trim the fat from your video, but you will refine your vision with music, sound, typography, and color. You'll use every trick in the book—this book, at least.

Since you recorded in a digital format (didn't you? DIDN'T YOU?), you have several options for editing that raw footage into something coherent and watchable. It's possible you already have a video editing program installed on your computer. Did you even bother to check?

No such luck? Well, as with cameras, it's more important to find an editing tool that's easy for you to use than it is to equip yourself with cutting-edge technology. If you can, get a hold of a free trial copy, or try out a friend's version, before you buy. That's what Guillermo del Toro does (I expect).

Whatever program you end up using, the process is similar: You excerpt individual snippets from the mass of video that you created, then drag them around to create a sequence to your liking. You can drag, can't you? Of course you can. Now, all you need to remember as you sculpt your masterpiece is what Hollywood moviemakers call "The Three K's."

THE FIRST **K: KEEP IT SHORT AND SWEET.**

Because of frequent browsing and tweeting, the viewers of your movie have the attention span of a gray squirrel. Their brains are unable to process more than a modicum of your cat's antics, no matter how clever those antics may be. So your video absolutely must engage viewers quickly, give them a positive feeling, stimulate them to share the video via social media, and then fade to black before their attention span resets itself and they move on to a slideshow about celebrity adoptions. You must accomplish this mission in roughly sixty seconds.

Impossible, you say? *Au contraire*, Pierre. Possible! Just follow this infallible structure:

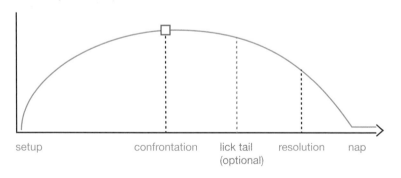

setup   confrontation   lick tail (optional)   resolution   nap

Arc of a Cat Video

ACT I: SETUP

Establish protagonist, his goal, and the main obstacle to success.

Elapsed time: 1–10 seconds

Example: Yarrcat, a scrawny tomcat in pirate getup, eyes treasure chest full of catnip on high shelf.

ACT II: CONFRONTATION

Protagonist confronts obstacles, testing his resolve.

Elapsed time: 10–45 seconds

Example: Yarrcat attempts to scale rigging to top shelf. Shark hand puppet pushes him off.

ACT III: RESOLUTION

Climax. Protagonist achieves goal, is permanently defeated, or otherwise resolves conflict.

Elapsed time: 45 seconds–1 minute

Example: Yarrcat leaps over shark, lands on treasure chest; cat and chest tumble to floor and contents spill everywhere. Approximately 10–20 cats dressed as sailors rush into scene and begin eating catnip. Trademark "YARRRRRR!" catchphrase displayed on screen in bright yellow letters.

THE SECOND K:
STYLE MATTERS, SO KEEP PILING IT ON

As the cat video market becomes saturated, it is incumbent upon directors to push visual boundaries in order to create a distinct, memorable style. For example, the enterprising director of *Henri, Le Chat Noir* decided on a somber black and white video effect. His cat was nothing to sneeze at, and the cinematography was jejune at best. But that director took Golden Kitty prize at the first-ever Internet Cat Video Festival in 2012. Henri's got an upcoming book, an endorsement deal with Friskies, twenty thousand Twitter followers, and a budding bromance with Christopher Walken. All because creator Will Braden went the extra mile and poured some style sauce onto the visual taco he'd created.

It's easy to add a signature look to your video by experimenting with the effects during the editing process. Consider these options:

EFFECT	RESULT
black & white	Hard-boiled detective cat
sepia	Western or Civil War cat
soft focus	Romantic lady cat
water ripple	Sea captain cat
x-ray	Doctor cat
fish eye	Stoned

gritty

old-timey

sexy

"You're as sweet as curdled cream, sister."

"This litter box ain't big enough for both of us."

"Kiss me! Kiss me, meow!"

moisty

x-rayey

trippy dippy zippy
ippy ippy zaaark
yappa zappa yaar

"The sea is a cruel mistress, yar."

"I have bad news: it looks like someone removed your balls."

"Where does my tail end, and where does I begin?"

And don't forget about transitions between scenes. The simplest is a basic cut, letting one scene start the instant the previous scene ends. That's jolting, though people will respect that you kept it real. But you might smooth the flow by inserting a fade or dissolve between scenes. There are many other possibilities, and each makes a statement: maybe a page curl (life is like a book!), clock wipe (tempus fugit!), a heart shape (awwwww), or a spinning cube (watch out! Cube!). Choose carefully.

THE THIRD K: ADD SOUND TO CREATE A VIDEO EVERYONE WILL REALLY LIKE.

People sure love to hear. And music can add drama to your clip, so it's tempting to grab toonage from your music library and create a rich, emotive soundtrack. But be careful: using copyrighted music can divert your cat's riches toward paying off hefty legal fees. So what's a poor cat videographer do? Well, you could try using the sound files that came with your editing software. Those are royalty free. I think. Actually, it's hard to tell, so you should probably read the fine print that came with the software . . . you know, the little booklet that you threw out.

Another option is to poke around online for music that's available under a Creative Commons license, which generally means "free music." (Technically it's "some rights reserved," so you should maybe see exactly what rights the artist is reserving before you go ahead and score that video.) If you have a budget to spend on sound—oooh, get a load of Mister Rockefeller over here—you can also buy royalty-free music and audio clips. You'll pay a one-time fee for unlimited rights to the material. That's not as good as free, but you're likely to find higher quality music, since somebody's actually being paid to compose it.

Maybe what you need is a basic laugh track, or some missile ground bursts. You know what global system of interconnected computers you can search to find a wide variety of free sound effect clips? That's right.

Finishing Touches

By now you've spent more hours with the video version of your cat than with the real thing. You even sent out for a pizza, then tried to make it arrive sooner by editing out the time in between. So why not push this thing out the door and reacquaint yourself with things you once took for granted, like sunlight and speaking in complete sentences?

Maybe walk away from the screen and come back after a good night's sleep. Invite a trusted friend or two to come by and preview the clip (they'll have to sign a nondisclosure agreement first, of course). Be open to feedback.

And finally, one last detail: You've got

Brand your video like a cattleman marking his prized steer.

a tiny piece of intellectual property—and it needs protection. So brand your video like a cattleman marking his prize steer. Use Photoshop or Illustrator to create a simple logo—maybe a tiny kitten with dollar signs for whiskers?—and tuck it into the corner of the video frame. You should also superimpose the address for your cat's website. You should also create your cat's website.

Ready to Upload!

Well, the moment has finally arrived. You're about to unleash a force that the world desperately wants but doesn't even realize it needs. Why, it's much like Alexander Fleming's discovery of penicillin. But how, you ask, will the fruit of your labor reach the awareness of millions?

I'll answer that question with a question: YouTube, ever heard of it?

Seriously, if you've never looked at YouTube, I'm not sure why you have a copy of this book. But, no judgment; maybe you were raised in one of those cults that forbids electricity in favor of beard growing and soap making. Maybe you just got out of prison. Whatever, Captain 2003.

So, YouTube is this premier online video-sharing website. It enables everyone to share their video clips with everyone else. The right video—yours, if you didn't screw it up somehow—can quickly gain millions of viewers and become a worldwide favorite. Perhaps I should have mentioned this sooner, but *this is the premise that your entire attempt at becoming incredibly wealthy kinda depends on.*

You'll need a YouTube account to upload videos, but signing up is easy. Just "log on" to your browser or whatever, go to YouTube.com, find the "New to YouTube" link, and follow all the prompts. Once you have your account, you can finally UPLOAD and SHARE the fruit of your labors! Uploading is as easy as hitting the upload button and choosing the clip. Which is totally what you should do, right now.

Stick a Fork in It, You're Done! (Not Really.)

Okay, video uploaded! Are you famous yet? Of course not. Because, surprise! There's more work to do. It's time to begin the crucial process of SHARING. This isn't like what you did in kindergarten, when you had five apple slices and little Jimmy didn't have any and Miss Grube made you give up two of yours and you got nothing in return. No, this version of sharing is more like grabbing people off the street and yelling in their ear until they cry. It's the kind of aggressive, intrusive, uncompromising marketing campaign that people love, and it has five equally important prongs.

Prong 1: Social media. Facebook, Twitter, Google+, LinkedIn, uh. . . Insta-something. Don't just invite groups of people to look at your videos—demand that they form a deep, emotional connection to this cat that can fill the void in their black and hollow hearts. Flood every social media platform you have access to and then join them all under a pseudonym and do it all over again.

Prong 2: Special-interest groups. Internet communities are nothing if not narrow and obsessive, so naturally there are online venues where people connect solely to swap opinions on all matters feline. Join and infiltrate these groups early, so that by the time you have a video to promote, you'll have built up enough "cred" to be taken seriously. A few to check out are Catster (recent post: "I missed my cat on vacation and my friends ridiculed me for it."), Catmoji (mission: "To make the Internet a better and happier place with cats."), and Purrsonals ("Where cat lovers meet and greet.").

> *Don't just invite groups of people to look at your videos—demand that they form a deep, emotional connection.*

Prong 3: Web presence. If your videos are the crack, and YouTube is the crack house, then www.yourcatsnamegoeshere.com is the street corner where you, the crack dealer, dole out vials to those pitiful addicts. We'll cover creating your own website or blog in the next chapter, but not in great detail, so don't get your hopes up.

Prong 4: E-mail. We all have friends and family who "go online" but lack the Web savvy to manage a Facebook profile or downvote a threadcrap. But those simple people shouldn't be ignored. Send them e-mails with direct links to your videos, explaining in clear text that they must click on the links if they want some meaning in their lives. Encourage them to pass the links on. Follow up with more e-mails.

Prong 5: Beyond YouTube. We've established YouTube as a video promised land for you and your cat. But don't overlook other video-sharing sites that cater to the 0.1% of Internet users who don't use YouTube. Examples include, oh, let's say Break.com, Vimeo.com, Metacafe.com, Dailymotion.com, and Stupidvideos.com.

How to Hijack a Search Engine

If a cat plays a keyboard in the forest and no one is there to hear it, does it make a sound? Who cares? The important point is this: *That cat will not earn one single dime.* So let's get your cat out of the forest of obscurity and into the forest of famousness, where she belongs.

Consider the typical cat-video enthusiast, trying to find the will to live until quitting time. Circumstances at the air traffic control room, 911 call center, or wherever this person works have allowed a few unsupervised moments. There's no time to lose! He attempts to zoom in on his favorite diversion with a few quick searches:

awesome cat video
funny cats
funniest cat video ever
cat make feel good about self

The search results come back in a flash. The man, in the mood for awesomeness or funniness, clicks according to his wont. Hilarity and/or awe ensues. Perhaps lives are saved. It's that simple! But with so many cat videos on the Net, how can you ensure that *your* video will be the one that gets all up in the grill of that MF's results page?

The answer: keywords. Search engines (those things you google with) glom onto these words like a pickpocket elephant sneaking peanuts from the zookeeper's trousers. YouTube and other video sites allow you to "tag" your video with whatever keywords you like. It's totally legit to copy the keywords from other successful cat videos, so start there. Eventually you'll want to come up with some on your own.

TYPE OF KEYWORD	EXAMPLE
Verbs and action words	jumps, destroys, cuddles
Movie and TV titles	Die Hard, Glee, Barton Fink
Descriptors	hilarious, awesome, hypercute
Celebrities and famous names	Lady Gaga, Aristotle, Homer Simpson
Funny or surprising props or objects in the video	sextant, teeter-totter, zune
Not really words	awwwwww, LOL, squeeeeee
Superlatives (the more superlative the better)	fattest, funniest ever, funniest cutest ever
Cats more famous than yours	Grumpy Cat, Bub, Yoruichi Shihoin
Current events	presidential election, salmonella poisoning, Golden Globes

Along with keywords, you'll also have to give your video a headline, a description, and tags (which are like keywords, but different, but who cares). For God's sake, the work goes on. Luckily, you can use your keywords in all of these slots. In fact, you should. Like the opposite of a three-year-old, the more you repeat something, the more attention a search engine will pay to it.

Title: You'll probably have only 100 characters to work with, so pack the title with as many keywords as will fit:

L'il Wayne the cat flies like Hurricane Sandy into bathtub. Hysterical!

Incredible kitten dances with glee after destroying origami shark. Awwwww!

Fattest cat named Madonna devours Gingrich-shaped potato. Awesome!!!!!

Courageous Egyptian cats protest invasion by Afghan puppy. Surprising!

Kitty cuter than Maru cuddles Kate Middleton lookalike. Unbelievable!

Description: Simply write a short entry that describes your video. Be as detailed and keyword dense as possible, with 800 words or so allotted. Include links to other videos, playlists, or your website.

Tags: Use your keywords here. Check out what's trending on Google, and see if you can apply any of those words as well. For example, if there's a stock market crash . . . well, in your video a cat "crashes" on the couch after taking "stock" of the salmon that you brought home from the "market." So it's legit!

White iPhone, broken screen

Super Bowl

Christina Hendricks, red-carpet meltdown

CHAPTER 4

The World Is Your Litter Box

Congratulations! People everywhere are talking about your cat. Things are really happening and you're shopping for a better cell phone to use in case someone actually returns your call. But as you ride that rocket to the top, don't ever forget that there's a younger, fresher kitty in a younger, fresher rocket right behind you. A cat who will happily throw you out of your rocket and watch your head explode in the vacuum of space just to take your place in the sun. Do you want to let that happen?

Thought not. To maintain a tight grip on fame and prosperity, you'll need a massive feline PR machine with more arms than an octopus. And each of those arms will need to sit in the driver's seat of a different fame-propelled rocket ship. So I present to you:

The Ten-Armed Octopus of Media Dominance

1. The Internet. Just as you used social media and the World Wide Web to bring your incredible feline to the world's attention, it's imperative that you keep using it to wedge the underpants of your cat's celebrity so deep into the world's ass-crack that it can never be shaken loose. Your biggest weapon here is your cat's website, ground zero for the wild-eyed cultists who are your cat's biggest fans.

How do you get a website, you ask? And how do you get that coveted www.mycatsname.com Web address? For crying out loud . . .

Well, maybe I haven't made it clear enough that this is a book for people who want to turn their cats into celebrities and then live off their fame forever, not a book for computer nerds whose idea of a good time is to sit in the basement writing "programs" for "Web pages." Surely you know someone who has her own Web page, so just ask that person what she did and then do that. The good news is that there are many services out there to help you build a website for free, albeit with limited options. Also, be aware that creating a website is a separate task from gaining use of the .com (or .net or .whatevs) domain name you want to use. If the name hasn't been taken, you can pay a small annual fee to a domain name registrar, which makes that name yours and yours alone. Most website makers will do that for you, too. And, good lord, could this topic become any duller? Let's move on.

You'll need to marshal your social media resources as well. Be sure your cat has a Facebook page, with no fewer than 200 friends. He should be liking and commenting frequently. Get him on LinkedIn, where he can network with other performing animals. Give the cat a blog so he (you understand I really mean you, right?) can post religiously about everything he does, every day. The blog and the Web page can be the same thing, and why wouldn't they be?

And your cat *must* have an active Twitter feed if he wants to stay relevant (unless Twitter's been replaced by something else by the time you read this book, like 3-D printing). Keep an eye on what's trending and get your cat's point of view out there:

#GayMarriage: Gay owners, straight owners, doesn't matter, just feed me.

#BirdFlu: Think i just ate a bird with h1n1!!! AAARRRRGGH

#NorthKorea: Kim Jong-un needs a good 18 hour nap #zzzzz #PMAO (=purring my ass off).

2. Merchandise. Shirts, hats, and novelties of all sorts bearing your cat's likeness and trademarked catchphrases—these are going to be your bread and butter. Don't waste time getting them out to a hungry public. But do consider your cat's image when deciding what to shill. Maybe your sweet baby kitten shouldn't be featured on a shot glass. Or maybe that's just crazy enough to work. Those college kids love their irony. And their Jägermeister. The truth is, whatever thing you can think of, there's somebody somewhere who will print your cat's face on it: pillows, filing cabinets, contraceptive devices, you name it. Find a vendor who will print a small batch and then see what sells.

gigantic floating pen?

whatever the
heck this is

pointless thingy

headless abomination
torso sheath

3. Public appearances. Crowds can be jarring for animals who tend to hate people. So it's important to condition your pet to enjoy being around her unwashed masses of fans. Start by appearing briefly at small venues, a Carl's Jr. or Kiwanis club. Misting adoring fans with fish oil will encourage your cat to interact with them. If all goes well, the two of you can move up to 4-H fairs, car dealerships, and, eventually, boat launches. Don't be afraid to make outrageous demands of bookers, like a fruit basket WITHOUT GRAPES, or a glass (not plastic!) bottle of organic 2% milk, chilled to no less than 38 degrees. This kind of entitlement will fuel your cat's celebrity like crazy.

4. Live events. Fashion shows, charity fund-raisers, gallery openings . . . your cat needs to see and be seen wherever people wear top hats and monocles. Make sure kitty has emptied his bowels and bladder before any outing to avoid red carpet mishaps. (You should do the same.) Invest in a trainer who will teach your kitty to walk slowly and allow the photographers a decent shot. Practice with flashes at home to eliminate the temptation to pounce.

5. Television. It's imperative that your cat make the talk-show rounds, so get yourself booked on whichever late-night shows mesh well with your cat's schedule. A friendly e-mail to the program's talent booker should be all you need to cement an appearance. Just insist that there be no other animal acts, or Jack Hanna, booked on the same night. Then leverage that appearance into a reality series (Nobody's Purr-fect! A chronicle of one pet's wacky road to fame!) and/or a guest spot on *Law and Order: SVU*

6. Charitable causes. It's about time your cat gave something back, isn't it? Nothing will cement his popularity like using his celebrity to champion a cherished cause. Kitten trafficking? Anti-declawing? Stricter dog control laws? It doesn't matter. Raising money and awareness are shrewd career moves. It makes your cat more likable and lends dimension to an otherwise shallow personality.

7. Product endorsements. This may be the sweetest octopus arm of all. Not only does endorsing a product get your feline's face in front of millions via a massive marketing campaign, you get paid as well! Don't make the mistake of being too selective. If you'd rather your cat not be associated with hard liquor, firearms, or prescription medications, just do what your favorite celebrities do: endorse potentially embarrassing products in ads that run in only non-English-speaking countries.

8. A book deal. Once you reach a certain level of fame, publishers will flock like vampire bats around a sleeping cow. Don't settle for the first offer to come along, though. Wait for a bidding war, and ask questions: How much is the advance? How much are the royalties? Demand the

famous
AUTHOR
ME OW
author's tale
LOOKING FOR HIS BOOK
CATNIP CIGARETTE
If your cat can't figure out how to use a computer, give him a typewriter

rights to all film and related merchandise, as well as editorial control (including cover art). What about the book tour? International rights? What kind of PR plan is in place? Just keep asking questions until you get bored, then take the deal from whoever's the most obsequious.

9. A movie deal. Let's be serious. What was the point of writing a book if you don't want it to be made into a movie? Besides, a movie is just a very long video, and your cat has done plenty of those. However, you must be hard-nosed to hammer out the best deal for your cat, because Hollywood is full of "sharks." Some tips: Get a summer release. Insist on a big-name director and a budget of at least $20 million. Demand script approval. And hold out for gross points on the back end. Use that exact phrase—you don't need to know what it means. And don't let them fool you with net points. Those are worthless.

10. Faking your cat's death. The world needs to imagine itself without your cat to truly appreciate his greatness. But you must perpetrate this hoax carefully. First, have a trusted third party open some e-mail accounts using a stolen laptop, and then register Twitter accounts under three different pseudonyms, at least one of which should reside in a country outside the continental United States. Next, have one of these "persons" wonder via social media if the "rumors" of your cat's demise are "true." Then have a second charlatan confirm the rumor, and have

the third do some tortured wailing about the senselessness of the loss. That should really get the tweets and retweets going! Meanwhile, stay silent until your publicist informs you that the news coverage is starting to slip. Then it's time to let someone glimpse your pet through a curtained window. Most fans will be overjoyed that their beloved idol is alive and well, while a lunatic fringe refuses to believe the evidence (bonus: their conspiracy theories will get your pet some press on slow news days).

My Cat Is an Internet Celebrity — Now What?

If you have followed this book's advice, you and your cat are now wealthy beyond your wildest dreams. Don't make the mistake of thinking your work is over, though. In the words of the Notorious B.I.G.: mo' money, mo' problems. In some way, Biggie must have known that his wealth and fame would soon present him with the biggest problem of all, that of the homicide victim. Will your cat face the same fate? Will you? No, and not necessarily. But while building a following, your cat will most certainly attract hordes of losers, all looking for a piece of *your* carefully realized dream. So it will be your job to pick them off like fleas.

People who claim to be . . .	are actually . . .
personal trainers	drug dealers
nutritionists	drug dealers
stylists	drug dealers
managers	pimps
accountants	thieves
acting coaches	waiters

But freeloaders and pushers are not the only issues you'll need to cope with during your cat's rise to stardom. Here are a few other pitfalls famous kitties must navigate in the high-stakes world of international fame.

Celebrity feuds. Naturally, you and your cat will be tempted to brag about his prowess with the opposite sex, about his money, his opulent lifestyle, and his superiority to other feline performers. This comportment is distasteful and unbecoming to a star. It's also what got Biggie popped.

Stay humble. If you must make uncharitable comments about another celebrity, choose someone who's wimpy and dead, like Don Knotts, or on the outs with the general public, like Mel Gibson. If you're going to kick someone, make sure they're already down.

Overexposure. Sift through the roles and endorsement offers carefully. It's tempting to cash in on every dollar you can. And it also makes good business sense. But the public is extremely fickle. In the time it takes to travel from one state fair appearance to the next, your kitty can go from HOT to NOT. Solution: long vacations.

Haters. They're gonna hate . . . it's what they do. So tell yourself and your kitty that those detractors are just broke-ass failures who don't have famous cats of their own or the ability to acquire any. If your cat seems depressed by the negativity, pet him.

Burnout. It can be frustrating trying to motivate your cat to push harder. You may be tempted to give her amphetamines "just once." Then pretty soon it's downers so she can sleep and crack on the weekends as a treat. That's an expensive way to keep on schedule! You're much better off to plan all shootings and appearances during the cat's two or three active hours. Don't try to work her round the clock, but do get endorsement deals for blankets, pillows, and bedding so she can sleep on the job.

Sibling jealousy. Other pets in your home may feel overlooked as you lavish attention on the superstar kitty. Soon they will ruin your carpets, and eventually a neighbor or relative will write a tell-all about your lousy parenting. Nip this problem in the bud by auctioning off any nonperforming pets. Make winning bidders sign a nondisclosure agreement forbidding them from cashing in on your famous cat's name.

Tabloid rumors. It's sad to think that those in your inner circle would stoop to selling stories about your cat to *Us Weekly.* But tabloids offer large sums for cat dirt. Wild speculation about pregnancies, addiction, and angry outbursts are to be expected. Just remember that any publicity is good publicity, and stick to the foolproof formula that all celebrities and politicians follow: deny, deny, deny, apologize.

Wild speculation about pregnancies, addiction, and angry outbursts are to be expected.

Stalkers. There are crazy people in the world—people who can't find meaning in personal relationships or successful cat-based careers. They need something to fill the terrible void. Your cat could be that thing—in fact, your entire financial future depends on your cat *being* that thing. But only as a *fantasy.* When a lady shows up in your home claiming to be the cat's wife, that's going too far. So invest in a solid security force before this happens. Mossad veterans are one option, as is putting old-timey shopkeeper bells on all your doors so nobody can sneak in without your knowledge.

Paparazzi. Relentless paparazzi are a drawback of fame, but they do help keep your cat in the public eye. So make sure your star kitty always looks her best when leaving the house, even if she's just going next door to poop in the neighbor's sandbox. You should always dress smartly as well; wear nice slacks at all times.

Catnip addiction. After a long day of shooting, with public appearances, photo ops, and maybe signing some "pawtographs" for her fan club, a cat may have trouble winding down. And before you know it, every day she's hitting the ol' 'nip (also known on the street as "flipnip," "the CN," "cat-coke," "purrrrb," "kitty jane," and "cracknip"). Keep your pet clean and sober by scheduling sensible workdays, with time for several naps, a healthy diet, and regular exercise to release kitty's natural endorphins. Reserve the cashizzle for occasional recreational use as permitted by law.

Unwanted pregnancies. Please, people, spay and neuter your pets. Baby mommas and baby daddies can take a significant bite out of your cat's earnings. A single litter can yield eight kittens! That's a lot of mouths for your cat to feed. And each of those kittens can have kittens of their own in just a few months. Your cat's amazing genes will spread through the feline population like wildfire, and sooner or later his signature traits will become commonplace and unmarketable. Plus, a sexually active cat is unlikely to get endorsement deals from family-friendly corporations like Disney, Sears, or UnitedHealth Group.

Mental breakdown. Not all cats are cut out for fame. In fact, as a species they're basically solitary low-key animals. But you wanted to drag the animal into the spotlight, and now there's a price to pay: your cat's emotional health. Frankly, it's your fault, and you should be ashamed. But don't panic. If the cat was found wandering the streets in a disoriented state or makes a spectacle of himself coughing up hairballs in a public place, your best bet is to blame it on dehydration. Issue an apology and get him out of the public eye. And six to nine months later, his inspirational against-all-odds comeback can begin.

My cat wants to fire me. So your cat wants to retain your personal relationship but would like to cut you out of his business dealings. That is called "pulling a Beyoncé," and you don't want to be caught off guard when your cat tries it. Beyoncé's dad should never have let his daughter marry a mogul like Jay Z. It cost him a child, a career, and a messy federal audit. Luckily, you have an ace in the hole that most parent-managers don't: Your cat is your legal property. Make sure you can support your claim with adoption records or a bill of sale, plus draw up some ironclad management contracts extending your complete control for the lifetime of the animal.

My cat has an attitude problem. Have you created a diva? Does your cat insist on gold flakes in his litter box or ground-up pearls in her

WARNING SIGNS

THAT YOUR CAT IS LOSING IT.

2. CRAZY EYES

3. EARS BACK

1. HISSING

	HAPPY	ANGRY
EAR	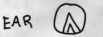	
EYE		
TAIL		

milk? Perhaps you've made the mistake of allowing your pet to feel irreplaceable. Solution: Pay a visit to the nearest animal shelter, to show that there are several fine kitties in those cages who would love to step right into your cat's life.

My cat wants to be emancipated. Does your cat vanish for days at a time, returning with milk on his whiskers and a collar you don't recognize? Do not allow your bread and butter to go "shopping" for a new family. If you've kept your paperwork in order, he has no chance of transferring his affections to some other household where no one will ask him to chase meatballs down the stairs or crawl into a flower pot on a daily basis. If needed, falsify documents to bolster your case.

Where Do My Cat and I Go from Here?

Sooner or later, even a super-successful impresario like yourself will have to admit that only so much can be done with one house cat. By carefully executing the principles outlined in this book, you likely bought yourself a few exhilarating years at the top of the netcat dogpile. And that's a pretty good ride for a Web star. The dancing banana thought the good times would go on forever, but where is he now? It's definitely not

It's never too late for a comeback!
Everyone thought Messiah Kitty's career
was over when he accidentally fell
asleep in the dryer, but three days later
his videos were more popular than ever!

peanut butter-jelly time any longer.

Is it over? In a way, yes. But in another, less factual way, no. For one thing, you can keep recording your cat's adorable antics and hoard the footage. Sooner or later, the public will be receptive to your cat's kind of talent once again, and when that happens, you don't want to get caught with your pants down. In the meantime, release those videos in a slow trickle, and you'll have enough footage to last well into your golden years. Fact: "Keyboard Cat" was shot in the 1980s but didn't become a sensation until two decades later. Who knows what wealth could have been accrued if the owner kept shooting and cataloging film? Indeed, cats are a timeless commodity.

Except that eventually even the most loyal fan will sicken of your particular cat. The blog traffic will dwindle; the comments will become half-hearted, even snide. *Snide*, after all the joy you gave to the world! Well, at least go out with some dignity. Announce your cat's retirement, plan a two-or three-year goodbye tour, and churn out a greatest hits reel and a coffee table book. Maybe start a foundation to fund a small museum dedicated to his career. Bide your time, and in a few years join a golden oldies Web troupe touring college campuses.

And what happens to you now that your cat is spent? Your dreams have been realized, and you can enjoy your well-earned riches and live life in the lap of luxury. Right?

I doubt it. Because you're a risk taker, and the kind of person who risks everything in the pursuit of cat-video-based wealth is not the kind of person to hold on to that wealth, even if things improbably work out. So I'm guessing you're hungry for the next challenge, partly because you thrive on adversity and partly because the grocery store won't extend you any more credit. Am I right? That being the case, let's close this treatise with some suggestions for your next exciting venture.

Manage a child star. You already know how to handle a short-tempered freak of nature whose brief career depends on superficial cuteness and a modicum of talent. So why not move on to the slightly higher rung on the ladder and work with a child actor? You'll have to abandon some techniques, like withholding food and making them sleep in a box. But others, like using a spray of water for negative reinforcement, will carry over quite nicely.

How about a goat? As this book goes to press, Google trend reports show a sharp spike in searches for goat videos. Goat searches have even *surpassed* cat searches, according to some reports. Plus, you can feed them tin cans and socks.

Try a sloth. Once regarded as a dull-witted symbol of laziness, the common sloth is increasingly considered cute, cuddly, and trendy. Pro: They won't run off set during a video shoot. Con: They may bite and maul you, albeit very slowly.

Get another cat. After all, why manage just one cat when you could build an entire empire?

eats tin cans

eats leaves

eats your dreams

eats the competition

A Gallery of Stars

The path to fame, glory, and financial independence via the Internet popularity of your cat may sometimes seem out of reach. But dozens of cats have achieved the upper echelon of success by employing the very practices outlined in this book. So whenever you're feeling defeated, just peruse this hallowed roster of famous feline talent. These cats are true heroes, and should be an inspiration to us all.

SOUPY THE NOODLE CAT

Real name: Tinky

When owner Ben Fritz of Lubbock, Texas, caught his mischievous tabby fishing noodles out of his bowl of chicken soup, his first reaction was, of course, rage. But when he recorded the scene with his smartphone to show to a behavioral therapist, he realized how entertaining a video of a cat covered in egg noodles could be. Since then Soupy the Noodle Cat has starred in over 200 Internet videos (who could forget "Won Ton Screwy") and recently landed a major endorsement deal with Tabatchnick Frozen Soup Singles.

SARCASTI-CAT

Real name: Clyde

Perhaps you've been the recipient of an e-card featuring Sarcasti-cat's image and one of his trademark sardonic comments: "Yeah . . . right" or "Smoooooth move, Einstein" or even "Meow. I really mean it this time." Look for his disdainful face on T-shirts, coffee mugs, and shower curtains everywhere. And watch for Sarcasti-cat's cameo appearance in the pilot episode of *CSI: Pet-Related Misdemeanor Unit.*

TWO-TAIL

Real name: Misty

Ann Wong of Carson City, Nevada, was stuck with a nondescript cat who seemed incapable of mustering any interesting behavior. But she didn't let that ability get in the way of her dreams; she simply clipped a fake tail onto her pet and lo! Two-Tail the double-appendaged cat was born. Ordinary cat behavior—eating, chasing a toy, sleeping—becomes incredibly fascinating when performed by a two-tailed cat, as Two-Tail's millions of fans can attest.

FLUFF

Real Name: Fluff

What do you do when your cat is so adorable that kids can't keep themselves from petting her, and so vicious that she clamps her jaws around the first chubby little finger to cross her sight line? Estelle Smith of Cricket, Ohio, turned a bloody negative into a lucrative positive by filming the results. Controversial and attention-getting, the Wrath of Fluff video series proves that carnage and cuteness do indeed mix.

GOOD BUDDY, THE TRUCKER CAT

Real Name: Paul

When you're haulin' a rig ten hours a day, it helps to have a companion who doesn't talk too much and can keep the rats away while you sleep. But when "Big" Ed Brown started sharing pictures of his tomcat via social media, Good Buddy the Trucker Cat became his ticket to an early retirement. Surely you've seen Good Buddy in one of his trucker caps featuring hilarious sayings like "I'd rather be vomiting hairballs" and "Same crap . . . different litter box."

RIGHT-SIDE-UP CAT

Real Name: Bella

Marsha Nutella had a dream: to train her cat to lie on her back with legs sticking straight in the air, so she could film her as "Upside-Down Cat." It was a sound plan, except that her uncooperative pet refused to learn her part. Some people would have given up at that point, but Marsha had a brainstorm: film the cat standing upright, then use editing software to turn *everything else* upside down. And with that began the storied saga of Right-Side-Up Cat, a lone champion who remains upstanding in a topsy-turvy world.

AFRAID OF BIRDS CAT

Real Name: Spazz

We can all identify with the misadventures of Afraid of Birds Cat. In his videos, he'll be going about his business: eating a snack, walking down the hall, licking his bum . . . when without warning his greatest phobia is triggered in the form of an avian interloper released into the scene. And as Afraid of Birds Cat bounces off walls and knocks over furniture in his panicked attempts to escape, we see reflected all of our own anxieties and fears. Oh, Afraid of Birds Cat, will you ever win? Will any of us?

GOODBYE KITTY

Real Name: Mittens

When Brenda Burrows of Hangnail, Florida, trained her cat Mittens to push doors closed on command, she changed her life forever. The clips of Goodbye Kitty slamming doors in people's faces went viral overnight, because who among us hasn't been tempted to end a boring conversation or annoying visit in just such a fashion? Religious proselytizers, census takers, dull neighbors, tedious in-laws—all have fallen victim to Goodbye Kitty's famous "closed door policy." And her famous catchphrase, "Goodbye and bad luck," is just icing on the cake.

Acknowledgments

We'd like to thank the following cats (and their agents, managers, publicists, and hairdressers) for lending their time and talent to this project. We wish you all fame, fortune, and nine lifetimes of powerful brand awareness.

Pages 2, 22, 45, and 56: Jeebus (Emily)

Page 6: Leo (April)

Pages 10, 17, 41, 85, 101, and 124: Snacks and Chaz (Jamie)

Pages 12, 33, 62, and 99: Bach and Handel (Eugene)

Pages 18 and 124: Luna and Raygun (Vince and Tara D.)

Pages 21 and 123: Lt. Ellen T. Ripley (Timaree and Carl)

Pages 25 and 122: Nigel and Rupert (Alix and Brian)

Pages 26, 54, and 64: Djuna and Zora (Rachel)

Pages 29, 39, and 59: Miko (Joelle)

Pages 30 and 39: Prudence (Tara H.)

Pages 34 and 69: Triscuit (Jerry)

Pages 39 and 66: Eliot (Christina)

Pages 39 and 106: Preta (Kerry)

Page 41: Cleo (Bobbi and Stephen)

Pages 41, 71, 76, and 125: Meemz and Boswell (Helen and Lucia)

Page 49: Lincoln (Bobbi and Matthew)

Pages 49 and 122: Smokey and Dexter (Linda and Larry)

Page 50: Durkadurkadurkadurka (Annie)

Pages 53 and 120: Owlbert (Poliana)

Pages 60, 78, 80, and 104: Abstract Cat and Inky Dink (Dustin)

Pages 65 and 97: Claude (Alex)

Page 68: Harper Lee (Lisa)

Page 72: Chops and Corn (dog) (Kay)

Page 75: Stevie (Megan)

Page 95: Oliver (Barry and Gina); Bootsie (Eleanor and Peter)

Pages 95, 121, and 123: Ronnie (Christine)

Page 108: Mewmerz (Kristina)

Page 113: Wally (Ilana and Jed)

Page 115: Astrid (Sarah)

Is Your Cat Ready for Her Close-Up?

$ $ $

Are You Ready to Cash In?

If you have enjoyed this book
or it has touched your life in
some way, we would love to
hear from you.

Please send your comments to:
P.O. Box 419034
Mail Drop 100
Kansas City, MO 64141
Or e-mail us at:
booknotes@hallmark.com